The Mind
& the Pen

copyright page

The Mind & The Pen
Written, edited and compiled by: Melody B. Evans
Cover art by: Melody B. Evans

Copyright © 2025 by Melody B. Evans

All rights reserved. No part of this publication may be reproduced, distributed or transmitted in any form or by any means, including photocopying, recording, or other electronic or mechanical methods, without the prior written permission of the publisher, except in the case of brief quotations embodied in critical reviews and certain other noncommercial uses permitted by copyright law.

Adherence to all applicable laws and regulations, including international, federal, state, and local governing professional licensing, business practices, advertising, and all other aspects of doing business in the US, Canada, or any other jurisdiction is the sole responsibility of the purchaser or reader.

Published and printed in the United State of America

Evans, Melody B., author.
The Mind & The Pen / by Melody B. Evans.
ISBN: 979-8-218-60378-6
Ebook ISBN: 978-1-300-48277-2
First Edition

author's note

This chapbook came from a time of self-doubt and writer's block. As I saw other poets around me, I wondered if I could even consider myself a "real" poet... but I am, and I'm reminded of that everyday.

No matter how long I go without writing, or how much I may struggle to finish certain poems, I know that poetry is truly life-giving and therapeutic, and a gift from God.

table of contents

Dedication	7
Mirror Mirror	9
Bars	11
Anticipation	13
Writer's Block	15
Critic	17
Still	19
Pen Wars	21
Trust The Process	23
All Along	25
The Pen	27
The Mind	29
Confessions Of A Poet	31
Survival Mode	35

Dedication

Alive...
that's how you make me feel.
When I hold you,
that's when my hidden thoughts are revealed.
It's like you bring out the best in me.
Even when I showcase the worst,
you still highlight the good
and teach me things about myself
I wouldn't otherwise see.
Without you in my life,
I don't know where I would be.
So thank you for the years you put up with me.
Like a high school sweetheart,
you're stuck with me.
Patient, you never rush me.
You wait until I'm ready to go,
so I know you were sent from above.
This is dedicated to the pen,
my first true love.

4-6-2023

Mirror Mirror

Mirror, mirror on the wall,
who's the flyest of them all?
Not me, you say?
That's fine,
cuz this poetry is a better reflection
that doesn't just show me myself,
but also shows me suggestions,
like the mind talks to the pen,
and before I know it,
I'm staring into the mirror of the mind.
It tells me I'm it,
and I don't deny the mind is dope,
but it also needs work.
That's where the pen comes in,
to show me how I love and how I hurt
so I can improve,
cuz the mirror shows my reflection,
but the notebook shows my truth.

Bars

They say my pen game is strong...
Well I've been doing some weightlifting.
Using pull-up bars to get these bars out,
then pull up and lay these bars down,
cuz bars get heavy.

Like gold bars,
I deliver these words for gold stars,
but you don't see the invisible scars
between my hands and the pen...

It taunts me.
Then I get writer's block and it haunts me.
I try to write and it feels daunting,
like, why do I even do it,
or... is it really therapeutic?

The pen talks to me,
like, "if I'm so good to you,
why did you neglect me?
If I comfort you so well,
why didn't you let me?"

They say the pen is mightier than the sword,
but my brain was mightier than the pen,
dictating what I wrote and how I wrote it.
Always had to have a title.
Rhyming every line
but not writing to unwind.
Then over time,
I let my mind take the back seat,
gave the pen the steering wheel,

turned off the GPS,
and let my mind reset
so these words could be fresh,
not stifled like Edith in *All In The Family*,
cuz the pen was the greatest gift
God could ever hand me.

Anticipation

So much to get out,
so little time...

I sound like the rabbit
and I'm not even in the hole,
just flying by on autopilot,
until I vomit these similes and metaphors
into a rhythm and flow for your ears to follow.

I feel no release, but it's coming,
like a major event we await in anticipation.
Fireworks from these fire words,
then boom, crackle, pop,
until the rhythm and flow stops.

The pen is always ready,
but the mind works in increments,
holding me back, but driving me forward
at different times, with different rhymes.
Never a steady beat,
but steadily helping me beat depression,
keeping me guessing when the next line will arrive.

Sometimes, it's not on my timing,
but the timing is always perfect,
cuz even in writer's block,
there's a lesson to be learned.
If it doesn't come naturally,
don't force it,
cuz force-fitting will always lead
to an uncomfortable position,
and my mission is to be free.

So as the ink drips freely from the tip,

taking me on a trip,
I embrace the journey,
cuz this winding road is no beaten path,
but the correct math with the right equation
to equal out on the other side.

This is my poetic roller-coaster ride.

Writer's Block

Writer's block...
where the mind blocks the pen from writing
and inciting genius lines
from appearing on a page,
so the mind fills with rage
with no way of escape,
because the mind and the pen won't cooperate,
and I'm left with blank paper and frustration.

I need some mental stimulation
before my mental goes numb
and the pen goes dumb,
cuz the paper is waiting on me
to unblock my mind
so the pen can fall in line
and follow behind.

4-26-2023

Critic

I criticize myself for not being able to write
when I haven't even picked up the pen.
I'm a writer that doesn't exercise
her right to compose...
A poet that pens poems
only to cleanse her soul.

But when the mic gets involved,
therapy can get washed out.
Instead of doing it for me,
now I'm doing it for you,
only to wonder why it's not fulfilling anymore.
I feel like I'm not winning anymore.

But it was never a game to begin with.
No win or lose,
but for some reason,
I had to prove to myself
I was good enough.

But I was always good enough,
pretending to be the judge in a slam
and I'm the only competitor...
But I don't have to be perfect,
as long as practice makes me better.

Still

My poetic mind is at a standstill...
still standing around
waiting for me to exercise my right
to write these lines,
but right now, all I know is how to scribble.

I've always been a stickler
for staying inside the lines,
and now, my mind refuses to come up with
enough metaphors to create them.
So I scribble my way into something coherent
with the hopes that soon,
I can create a masterpiece from this abstraction,
with satisfaction to follow.

Until then,
my poetry stands still...
still waiting for me to put pen to the page,
from letters to words to phrases.
These are the stages of sanity.

Pen Wars

Mind jumbled.
Thoughts playing hopscotch across my brain.
Pen in hand, but the words don't seem to land.

Click on, click off, click back on again.
Writing the date,
hoping the movement will inspire,
but the desire to quit
after three minutes of nothingness is strong.

The force is not with me.
I am no Jedi.
This lightsaber of a pen is faulty.
The wars of being a star and just a writer haunt me,
but being a writer is just fine...
as long as I can write,
because a star can explode,
and I wanna remain calm in every storm,
so I make waves with the pen,
controlling the tide.
Breathe in, breathe out, breathe in again.

I've been told I'm dope,
I just need it to seep in,
rushing through my veins,
traveling to my heart
so I know without a doubt
that this drug is worth it.

The pen isn't perfect,
but it provides a service
of therapeutic expression
and lessons to get me through life
for as long as I'm on Earth's surface.

9-28-2024

Trust The Process

They tell me to trust the process,
and while I still don't know what that means,
I proceed to do the only thing I know how
in the most honest way possible,
which is write my heart.
The part of me I don't want you to see
is the very thing that pushes me forward,
even though sometimes
I wanna ignore it and hide,
it seems the pride my pen provides
goes to the mind,
as though I'm moving mountains with each letter.
So for better or worse,
I vow to let the pen tap into my mind
and reveal the real
until the last of the ink drops,
which won't be until my heart stops.

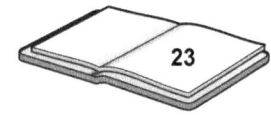

All Along

Like a comic strip,
these thought bubbles appear,
except they're empty,
void of imagination in this age of information,
and full of impatience, regardless of the situation.

I've run out things to say,
so the pen has nothing to jot,
just dot after dot until an ellipsis forms.
To be continued...

Thoughts seeking another venue, or avenue.
Whichever way you look at it,
an escape is necessary,
cuz this jail cell of writer's block has me blocked in...
or blocked out...
I can't really tell anymore.
Can't tell if these thoughts are icing me out,
like how dare I think,
have the audacity to imagine,
or muster up the courage to compose.

I'm an artist, but the art ain't flowing.
Motivation, non-existent,
inspiration seems distant,
but I'm persistent.
Never letting go, I'm on a mission.

Objective: write some words that go together,
no pressure, no timer,
just words on page.

Don't be concerned about what to do on stage
cuz this isn't a performance, it's a vent session.
This is just to see if you get past the first lesson.
So pick up the pen and write
the first thing that comes to mind,
and if you wanna spice it up,
you can even throw in a rhyme,
a metaphor here and there,
some alliteration to follow,
and you'll realize all along,
these thoughts were never hollow,
and before you know it,
you've got a whole cohesive poem.
Congratulations, you're a poet.
Well... you were a poet all along.

The Pen

A force to be reckoned with,
but am I really?
Aspiring to be like the poets I see,
but neglecting to see the poet in me.

I be writing,
but sometimes, me and the pen be fighting.
It tells me to lighten up
and write from the heart,
but the mind plays tricks on the pen,
so writer's block takes over
until it's ready to leave, and by then,
I got so much up my sleeve
that I don't know where to begin.
Just begin...
until eventually, the mind gives in to the pen,
cuz the pen always wins in the end.

3-19-2023

The Mind

This mind is a gold mine,
I just haven't struck yet,
but it's coming.
Becoming the poet I know I can be,
the pen and pad holding me accountable.
Feats that seem insurmountable,
more powerful than my mind can handle,
yet the pen prompts me.

Even when these thoughts taunt me
and writing seems daunting,
I know I'll never find the treasure that lies beneath
if I don't put in the work to search for it.

They say the mind is a terrible thing to waste.
Well I refuse to waste away,
dismissing my gift as just another play thing,
cuz I say things in a way that only I can say it,
then replay it at full volume
until it sinks in.

These words are golden,
bold enough to cross my mind
at the right time with the right rhyme,
because rhyming with Divine timing
is sure to remind me
that I don't have to be a star to keep shining.
I just have to turn the light on.
Whether it's a lamp or a flashlight,
I refuse to gaslight myself
into thinking I'm less than dope.

I'm a poet and I know it,
so I show it like I show you this brown skin.
I'm grounded.
So when I strike gold,
don't ask me how I found it.
Just know I tapped in with the pen,
prospecting these words until poetry presented itself on this paper for you to savor...
because this mind is a gold mine,
so whether these words consist of nouns or verbs,
I'm rich with the gift God gave me,
forever grateful that He used poetry to save me.

Confessions Of A Poet

I'm a poet:
I expose myself without ever shedding my skin
and reveal parts of me
I really don't want you to see
in an attempt to gain clarity.

This clarity is my inner therapy,
so think twice
before you offer unsolicited advice
or make comments about my life,
cuz this is MY pen's sacrifice:
to transfer tears into ink,
and thoughts into a masterpiece
that you can snap to,
so when life throws a snafu,
I bleed all over this notebook so well,
you would think I had the sauce,
no Ragu.

The rush that I feel when I step to the mic
is unlike any other,
turning this introvert into a
three-minute public speaker,
eager to make you listen
and stroke my ego,
until a first round elimination
Deebo's me back to humility.

Losing all focus,
I notice when competition takes over,
more concerned with winning a slam
than showing you who I really am,
and letting therapy escape me like a thief,
robbing me of my peace,

until I retreat back into the notebook,
confessing my sins with the pen
so I can breathe again.

This is what breathing feels like:
inhaling thoughts,
exhaling clever lines that rhyme,
using alliteration to provide poetic peace,
prompting you to hear past what my mouth speaks
cuz I am more than these words,
I'm the whole poem.

This poem is what I say it is,
wondering if there's purpose in this poetry,
I pray it is,
because prayer is what got me here:
an attempt to escape depression,
turned into therapeutic expression
and a lesson that poetry is life.

And life is worth living,
not merely existing,
wandering around aimlessly,
a rebel without a cause,
so I rebel against depression with the pen,
causing myself to press on to the end
because poetry is passion.

This passion can't be stifled,
muted or knocked down,
cuz I've been awakened
like a bear out of hibernation
and sleep is no longer an option,
so I stay woke,
like a hotep on my conscious tip,
no more tip-toeing,
I create conflict with each rhyme I spit,

so before you count me out,
consider this:
even if these lines don't seem to hit,
they never miss,
you just weren't the intended target.

So instead of feeling like a failure,
longing for snaps and "rewinds,"
I let this passion light a fire under my behind
to move ahead.

Cuz I'm a poet,
so whether I slam,
or simply stand before you,
exposing my soul for your approval,
just know that this is my therapy.
So before you go comparing me,
ranking me with the others,
just know that I strive for
purpose over popularity,
and with all sincerity,
I do this for me, not you,
so even if I never make bread,
I don't need to be the next Sara Lee,
I just need to be the best poet I can be:
Melody.

Survival Mode

This is not a hobby.
This is survival.
Pre-apocalyptic therapy
for the post-apocalyptic reader,
eager to breathe life into a world of walking dead,
because poetry never dies.

It grows like a rose from the concrete,
more concrete than the rose itself,
never withering,
it stands strong without soil
and doesn't need water to survive.
It stays alive.

It doesn't need help.
The pen and pad are just tools,
but a poem can write itself.
Spoken words preferred over manuscripts,
yet the script is necessary,
a written picture of the mind that, in time,
will become as timeless as a Van Gogh original,
because how else do you go from
David in the Psalms
to a slam competition
if it wasn't relevant all along?

Poetry is alive and thriving,
necessary for survival,
but more than just surviving.
It turns madness into a masterpiece
and depression into dopeness,

sadness into sonnets
and pain into purpose,
all with the swipe of a pen,
or the type of a key.

So what is poetry to me?
Life.

The pen is my hoe,
the paper is the soil,
planting seeds of ink
and watering them with vulnerability.

This garden of scribble scrabble
isn't a game you can spell out,
not a puzzle you can piece together,
because I am already whole.

This garden will grow into a greenhouse,
full of the finest fruit,
because genetic modification
will never be as good as the real thing.

AI can't write this,
can't mold my emotions into a masterpiece
the way honesty and natural intelligence can.

I'm proud to say this is home-grown,
because after all,
once the world ends,
we all turn into farmers fighting to flourish
in the face of famine.

So I might as well get a head start
with fresh ink to foster these first fruits,
cuz this isn't a hobby,
this is survival,
and I just want to live forever...

about the author

Melody B. Evans is a poet, spoken word performer, and graphic designer, originally from St. Louis, Missouri. She started writing poetry at the age of 14 and fell in love with the art form.

Melody attended the illustrious Claflin University and fully supports the institution of HBCUs. Undergrad is where she discovered her love for music and learned how to create, record and produce music. She has released four EPs and one full-length album, available on all major streaming platforms: Apple Music, Tidal, Spotify, Amazon Music, and Deezer, and available for purchase on Bandcamp.

Melody (aka The Official Melody) is also the host of online-based radio show Overseas Dreams Radio, the best radio show on Earth and in space! She plays music from multiple genres, from all over the world, and interviews poets, singers, rappers, producers and DJs. Listen to Overseas Dreams Radio on Soundcloud, Mixcloud, and YouTube @overseasdreamsradio.

While she has lived in several places over the years, she still claims St. Louis as her hometown, and represents the Midwest wherever she goes.